PUSHES & PULLS

Authors

Mary Atwater
The University of Georgia

Prentice Baptiste
University of Houston

Lucy Daniel
Rutherford County Schools

Jay Hackett
University of Northern Colorado

Richard Moyer
University of Michigan, Dearborn

Carol Takemoto
Los Angeles Unified School District

Nancy Wilson
Sacramento Unified School District

Pushes and pulls in your
everyday world

Macmillan/McGraw-Hill School Publishing Company

MACMILLAN / McGRAW-HILL

SCIENCE TURNS MINDS ON™

CONSULTANTS

Assessment:

Janice M. Camplin
Curriculum Coordinator, Elementary Science
Mentor, Western New York
Lake Shore Central Schools
Angola, NY

Mary Hamm
Associate Professor
Department of Elementary Education
San Francisco State University
San Francisco, CA

Cognitive Development:

Dr. Elisabeth Charron
Assistant Professor of Science Education
Montana State University
Bozeman, MT

Sue Teele
Director of Education Extension
University of California, Riverside
Riverside, CA

Cooperative Learning:

Harold Pratt
Executive Director of Curriculum
Jefferson County Public Schools
Golden, CO

Earth Science:

Thomas A. Davies
Research Scientist
The University of Texas
Austin, TX

David G. Futch
Associate Professor of Biology
San Diego State University
San Diego, CA

Dr. Shadia Rifai Habbal
Harvard-Smithsonian Center for Astrophysics
Cambridge, MA

Tom Murphree, Ph.D.
Global Systems Studies
Monterey, CA

Suzanne O'Connell
Assistant Professor
Wesleyan University
Middletown, CT

Environmental Education:

Cheryl Charles, Ph.D.
Executive Director
Project Wild
Boulder, CO

Gifted:

Sandra N. Kaplan
Associate Director, National/State Leadership
Training Institute on the Gifted/Talented
Ventura County Superintendent of Schools Office
Northridge, CA

Global Education:

M. Eugene Gilliom
Professor of Social Studies and Global Education
The Ohio State University
Columbus, OH

Merry M. Merryfield
Assistant Professor of Social Studies and Global
Education
The Ohio State University
Columbus, OH

Intermediate Specialist

Sharon L. Strating
Missouri State Teacher of the Year
Northwest Missouri State University
Marysville, MO

Life Science:

Carl D. Barrentine
Associate Professor of Biology
California State University
Bakersfield, CA

V.L. Holland
Professor and Chair, Biological Sciences
Department
California Polytechnic State University
San Luis Obispo, CA

Donald C. Lisowy
Education Specialist
New York, NY

Dan B. Walker
Associate Dean for Science Education and
Professor of Biology
San Jose State University
San Jose, CA

Literature:

Dr. Donna E. Norton
Texas A&M University
College Station, TX

Tina Thoburn, Ed.D.
President
Thoburn Educational Enterprises, Inc.
Ligonier, PA

Macmillan/McGraw-Hill School Division
10 Union Square East
New York, New York 10003

Printed in the United States of America

ISBN 0-02-274263-8 / 3

2 3 4 5 6 7 8 9 VHJ 99 98 97 96 95 94 93 92

Amusement park in Germany

Mathematics:

Martin L. Johnson
Professor, Mathematics Education
University of Maryland at College Park
College Park, MD

Physical Science:

Max Diem, Ph.D.
Professor of Chemistry
City University of New York, Hunter College
New York, NY

Gretchen M. Gillis
Geologist
Maxus Exploration Company
Dallas, TX

Wendell H. Potter
Associate Professor of Physics
Department of Physics
University of California, Davis
Davis, CA

Claudia K. Viehland
Educational Consultant, Chemist
Sigma Chemical Company
St. Louis, MO

Reading:

Jean Wallace Gillet
Reading Teacher
Charlottesville Public Schools
Charlottesville, VA

Charles Temple, Ph. D.
Associate Professor of Education
Hobart and William Smith Colleges
Geneva, NY

Safety:

Janice Sutkus
Program Manager: Education

National Safety Council
Chicago, IL

Science Technology and Society (STS):

William C. Kyle, Jr.
Director, School Mathematics and Science Center
Purdue University
West Lafayette, IN

Social Studies:

Mary A. McFarland
Instructional Coordinator of
Social Studies, K-12, and
Director of Staff Development
Parkway School District
St. Louis, MO

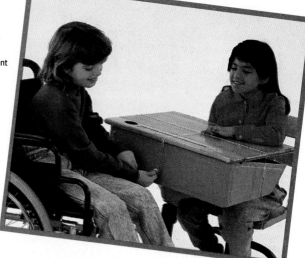

Students Acquiring English:

Mrs. Bronwyn G. Frederick, M.A.
Bilingual Teacher
Pomona Unified School District
Pomona, CA

Misconceptions:

Dr. Charles W. Anderson
Michigan State University
East Lansing, MI

Dr. Edward L. Smith
Michigan State University
East Lansing, MI

Multicultural:

Bernard L. Charles
Senior Vice President
Quality Education for Minorities Network
Washington, DC

Cheryl Willis Hudson
Graphic Designer and Publishing Consultant
Part Owner and Publisher, Just Us Books, Inc.
Orange, NJ

Paul B. Janeczko
Poet
Hebron, MA

James R. Murphy
Math Teacher
La Guardia High School
New York, NY

Ramon L. Santiago
Professor of Education and Director of ESL
Lehman College, City University of New York
Bronx, NY

Clifford E. Trafzer
Professor and Chair, Ethnic Studies
University of California, Riverside
Riverside, CA

STUDENT ACTIVITY TESTERS

Jennifer Kildow
Brooke Straub
Cassie Zistl
Betsy McKeown
Seth McLaughlin
Max Berry
Wayne Henderson

FIELD TEST TEACHERS

Sharon Ervin
San Pablo Elementary School
Jacksonville, FL

Michelle Gallaway
Indianapolis Public School #44
Indianapolis, IN

Kathryn Gallman
#7 School
Rochester, NY

Karla McBride
#44 School
Rochester, NY

Diane Pease
Leopold Elementary
Madison, WI

Kathy Perez
Martin Luther King Elementary
Jacksonville, FL

Ralph Stamler
Thoreau School
Madison, WI

Joanne Stern
Hilltop Elementary School
Glen Burnie, MD

Janet Young
Indianapolis Public School #90
Indianapolis, IN

CONTRIBUTING WRITER

Barbara Keeler

Pushes and Pulls

Lessons   **Themes**

Activities!

Features

Links

Departments

Pushes and Pulls

Superheroes have superpowers. Some of them can fly and leap over buildings. Superheroes are much stronger and more powerful than a real person. When they fall or get hit by something, they aren't hurt as a real person would be. Who are some of the superheroes you know about?

Sometimes a superhero story is based on the life of a real person. The person might be very strong or wise or skilled. People start telling stories about the person. Soon the stories aren't real any-more. In the stories, the person is doing things that a human being couldn't do. But the stories keep growing, and before long, a superhero is invented. These superhero stories are a way of showing respect and admiration for the real person.

More than 100 years ago, a man named John Henry worked as a steel driver for the Chesapeake and Ohio railroad.

John Henry was so strong he could do the work of two people. He did his job better than anyone else. The people who worked with him saw how strong and skilled he was.

Once John Henry raced against a machine called a steam drill to see which one could work faster.

Here are some of the words of a song people made up about him.

The man that invented the steam drill,
He thought he was mighty fine,
But John Henry he made fourteen feet
While the steam drill only made nine,
The steam drill only made nine.

No real person is a superhero. But with the right machines, you can do almost anything a superhero can do.

Hydraulic lift

There are machines that can help lift heavy objects, like a car or truck.

There are machines that can smash through walls and buildings, too.

Wrecking ball

There are machines that make it possible for you to fly.

Minds On! Think of two things that your favorite superheroes do. In your *Activity Log* on page 1, make a list or draw pictures of machines that help us do the same things. ●

Twin-propeller airplane

Machines are useful for many things. Of course, they can't do anything by themselves. They require energy (en´er jē) to run. **Energy** is the ability to make things move.

Sometimes a person supplies the energy a machine uses.

Olympic bike racers

Sometimes the energy comes from electricity or from burning coal or oil. Where does the energy come from to run the machines that you listed in the Minds On activity?

Coal

FUEL OIL

Fuel oil

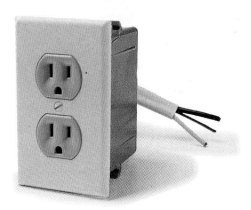

Electrical Outlet

In this unit, you'll find out more about the energy you supply through pushes and pulls to make things move. You'll also see how simple machines help us do some of the things superheroes do.

Science in Literature

Books can help us see things in a new way. Some of the tools you use every day are examples of the machines you are learning about.

The Berenstain Bears' Science Fair

by Stan and Jan Berenstain.
New York: Random House, 1977.

"Big or small or in between, if it helps you do work, then it's a MACHINE!" When the Berenstain Bears get ready to make science projects, they have to learn a lot about just what you are going to be learning about in this unit. See if you can find a project you might like to do when you read this book.

Looking Inside: Machines and Constructions
by Paul Fleisher & Patricia A. Keeler.
New York: Atheneum, 1990.

If you've ever wished you had "X-ray vision" and could see inside things, this is the book for you. You'll see what's inside a piano, a pay telephone, an escalator, a camera, and many other items. This "inside view" will help you understand how they work.

Other Good Books To Read

Muscles to Machines
by Neil Ardley.
New York: Gloucester Press, 1990.

This book shows you how much you can do using simple machines. It has many pictures, projects, and points about using them.

Pyramid
by David Macaulay.
Boston: Houghton Mifflin Company, 1975.

The Egyptian pyramids are one of the Seven Wonders of the World. How did people who lived 3,000 years ago build these amazing structures?

The Extraordinary Invention
by Bernice Myers.
New York: Macmillan Publishing Company, 1984.

Sally and her father are inventors. This is the story of their extraordinary invention that doesn't work quite right.

"Push on — keep moving!"
— *Thomas Morton*

Runners in 100-meter race

From Here to There

People are always moving from one place to another. Some people have breakfast in New York and dinner in San Francisco! People have traveled to the moon and walked on it. Spacecraft have passed near most of the planets in our solar system. All these trips are possible because of what people have learned about why and how things move.

Minds On! What paths do you travel at school? Where are you in the morning? At lunch? At the end of the day? In your *Activity Log* on page 2, draw a map of the places to which you move during the day.

In a moment, you will move the page of this book. Then you'll prove that some objects moved by looking at their positions. ●

Activity!

Huff and Puff!

What makes an object move? In this activity, you will find out how we know things move.

What You Need

paper

meter tape

Activity Log pages 3-4

pencil

masking tape

wood block

What To Do

1 Mark a starting line on the table with a short piece of masking tape. Line up the block, the ball of paper, and the pencil on the starting line.

2 Predict what will happen if you blow each object using one puff of breath. Write your predictions in your *Activity Log*.

3 Blow each object using one puff of breath. **Note:** Try to use the same amount of breath each time you blow an object. Mark where the object stops with a piece of masking tape. Write the name of each object on the tape.

4 Record in your *Activity Log* your observations of what happened to each object. Measure the distance each object moved. Draw a picture showing the starting place and where each object ended up.

What Happened?

1. Which of the objects moved?
2. Which object moved the farthest?
3. Which object moved the fastest?
4. Draw a graph of the results of each movement.

What Now?

1. Why do you think one object moved farther than another?
2. What would have happened if you had blown harder?
3. What was the connection between the fastest object and the one that moved farthest?
4. How did the objects move? Did they spin, go straight, or do something else?

EXPLORE

Where Is It?

In the activity, when you blew on the objects, they moved. You know they moved because you saw where they started and where they stopped. Even though you blew about the same for each object, they didn't all move the same distance.

Each of the objects was in a certain position (pə zish´ ən). **Position** is what we call the place where something is. Right now, your position is probably in your seat.

In baseball, you play a certain position. This means you stay in a certain place during the game. What positions do you see here? What position do you like to play?

An object is always somewhere. Whether it is still or moving, it always has a position. When something is moving, its position keeps changing.

When you take a picture of something moving like this skateboarder, the picture is a record of its position at one moment.

Without position, you couldn't give directions to your home. You couldn't tell someone where to look for anything.

Have you ever played the game of Hot and Cold? You direct someone to find something by saying, "You're getting warmer!" You're talking about position when you do this.

When you describe an object's position, you compare it to the position of another object. How would you tell someone to get from the mailbox to the X? Is there more than one way?

TRY THIS Activity!

Hidden Treasure

In this activity, you will direct a partner to an object using position.

What You Need
Activity Log page 5

Imagine that an object in your classroom is a hidden treasure. Draw a treasure map with directions that tell how to find the object. Choose a spot in the room as a starting point. Say how far away and in what direction the treasure is. Describe how high it is from the floor. Exchange directions with a partner, and find each other's treasures. Record any problems you had in following the directions. Discuss these and make suggestions for improving each other's directions.

Motion

Motion (mō´ shən) is what happens when something changes its position. All motion takes time to happen. Some things change position in very little time. When you throw a ball to a classmate, it gets there in only a few seconds. Some things move so fast you don't even see them move. Other things move so slowly that they seem to be sitting still.

The wings of a hummingbird in flight move so fast that all you see is a blur. Part of the reason hummingbirds can hover by flowers is because their wings beat so fast.

Music/Art Link

Moving Pictures

Artists can draw a picture of only a single moment in time. A picture isn't like a movie where you can see an object change positions. On page 6 in your **Activity Log,** draw a picture of something that is moving. How can you show that the object is in motion? Look at the pictures in this lesson to get some ideas.

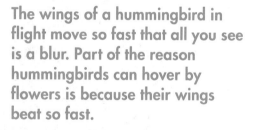

18

Clouds do not seem to move very fast, but they do move. Flowers open and close. Leaves turn toward the sun.

Parts of Earth's surface move very slowly, too. You'd have to measure very carefully to see how much they move in an entire year. Scientists do just that to find out more about how Earth moves and changes.

Even when you're resting, you're moving a little. You move when you breathe!

Minds On! Look at the hour hand on a clock. Is it moving? On page 7 in your *Activity Log,* draw a clock to show when school starts. Then draw another clock to show when you go to lunch. How do you know the hand moves? ●

Motion can be observed and measured. It's very hard to see the hour hand on a clock move. But you can record its position at different times. Then you can use your records to measure how far it has moved.

Activity!

Speed Ball

What You Need
2 balls exactly alike, *Activity Log* **page 8**

Hold one ball, and give one to a classmate. Stand with this person about 10 feet from a wall. Have a third person say "Go!" Throw one ball underhand gently toward the wall, and roll the other ball toward the wall. Which ball reached the wall first? Why? Try this two more times to see what happens.

Biker slowing to a stop.

Speed

Speed (spēd) is the measure of how fast an object moves. In the activity, the ball you threw moved faster. It had a greater speed so it took less time to get to the wall. The other ball had a slower speed and took longer to travel the same distance.

Speed is stated in different ways. But each one uses a distance measure and a time measure.

Motion can be changed as well as measured. Starting, stopping, speeding up, slowing down, and changing direction are all changes in motion.

In the United States, miles and hours are used to show speed. In most other countries, people use kilometers and hours. You can use any distance and time measure you want to show speed.

SPEED LIMIT 55

How Far and How Fast?

In the United States, most people use cars, buses, trains, boats, or airplanes to go from one place to another. Each moves safely at different speeds. Safety is one reason we measure the speed of cars and buses. A speed limit is the highest safe speed the law allows. What are the speed limits where you live?

Freeway entrance and exit ramps

CAREERS

Go With the Flow

Transportation engineers help people keep moving. They plan highways, airports, and railway and bus systems. When roads get too crowded, a transportation engineer might plan more lanes on some of the roads. A bus system and a subway would help, too. What types of transportation are used in your community?

To be a transportation engineer, you have to go to college for four years. In college you'll learn about road planning, technical drawing, and lots of science.

Most animals wouldn't have any problems staying under the speed limit. Other animals would break speed laws if they could run or fly at top speed for long periods of time. Look at the top speed for each animal below. None of them could move at top speed for very long. Which one would win a race?

Ostrich 65 kilometers (about 40 miles) per hour

Peregrin falcon 290 kilometers (180 miles) per hour when diving

Human 33 kilometers (about 20 miles) per hour

Giant tortoise 0.25 kilometer (about 0.15 mile) per hour

Miles Per Hour

You can use speed limits to help predict how long a trip will take. It's about 400 miles from San Francisco to Los Angeles. How long would it take if you drove 55 miles per hour? How long would it take if a train went 70 miles per hour or an airplane flew 200 miles per hour?

Sum It Up

You have a position, and so does everything you see. If something is in motion, its position is changing. We can tell it moves because its position changes compared to something else. You can compare how fast things move by finding their speeds.

Spider 1.62 kilometers (about 1 mile) per hour

Critical Thinking

1. You tell your dog to sit and stay. Then you leave the room for a minute. How can you tell if your dog moved?

2. Your cousin lives 1,000 miles away, so you can't race together. How could you find out who was faster?

3. How could you find out how fast you walk?

Life is full of pushes and
pulls. Some are large and
some are small. How many
pushes and pulls do you see
in this picture? Are some
larger than others? How can
you tell?

Push and Pull

Push. Pull. How many times a day do you push or pull something? You may start out by brushing and flossing your teeth. You push the toothbrush. You pull the dental floss. You push your door open, and you pull it closed. What pushes you or pulls you? When you jump in the air, what pulls you down? Does something push you or pull you to school? Can you move without pushing or pulling?

Minds On! Lift the page of your book. Did you pull it or push it? ●

After you turn the page, you will have a chance to measure some pushes and pulls.

Activity!

Large or Small?

In this activity, you will be pushing and pulling things around you. You will also measure the force it takes to move some common objects.

What You Need

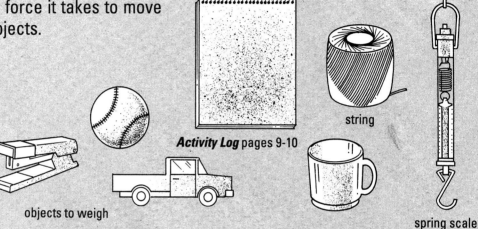

objects to weigh

Activity Log pages 9-10

string

spring scale

What To Do

1 Hook your finger in the spring scale, and pull gently while another person holds the other end of the scale. A newton (nū´ tən) is a unit used to measure pushes and pulls. Make the scale read 10 N. Does it matter who pulls? Record and draw your observations.

2 Push against the hook of the spring scale. Make the scale read 10 N. Does it matter how either of you pushes? Record your observations.

3 Use the string and spring scale to pull and then push some objects in your classroom. Be sure to pull at a steady speed. Record what the spring scale reads for each object. How is this like pushing or pulling against another person?

4 Pull the wheeled object. How many newtons does it take to start it moving? How many does it take to keep it moving? Record your observations.

What Happened?

1. What did you feel when the other person pushed or pulled on the spring scale?

2. Which objects made the scale read the highest when you pulled them?

What Now?

1. Both pushing and pulling made the spring scale read 10 N. How are pushing and pulling the same?

2. Why did it take a bigger pull to move some objects?

EXPLORE

Forces

The spring scale measured pushes and pulls. The harder you pushed or pulled, the greater the number of newtons the scale showed. A **newton** is a unit that measures forces. It took a bigger pull or push to move heavier objects at a steady speed.

All pushes and pulls are **forces** (fôrs´ əz). Without forces you couldn't live as you do now. You get up in the morning by pulling or pushing yourself out of bed. Could you open a door without force? What forces do you use to do simple jobs?

You use energy to create some forces. Energy is the ability to make things move. How do you get energy to make things move?

How many pushes and pulls do you see in this picture? Who is pushing? Who is pulling? Who is doing both?

When you lean (push) against something, the thing you are leaning against is pushing back with an equal amount of force.

Minds On! Think about how you use force. Move your desk forward a little. Move it back to you. How did you use force? Close your book. Did you push or pull? Open it. Did you push or pull? ●

Even though all forces push or pull, there are different kinds of forces. Some act between objects that are not even touching. To see a force like this, do the Try This Activity.

Activity!

Jumping Clip

What You Need

magnet, wad of paper the size of your finger, meter tape, paper clip, *Activity Log* page 11

Put the magnet on your desk. Place the paper clip 1 cm away from it. What happened? Now put the wad of paper 1 cm away from the magnet. What happened? Record your observations.

The paper clip probably moved and stuck to the magnet. The paper didn't move. Magnets pull on certain kinds of metals. The forces between them are pulls. Even though they aren't touching, they pull on each other. There are other forces that pull between objects whether they're touching or not. One of these forces is pulling on you right now. Do you know what it is?

Gravity

Gravity (grav´ i tē) is the force of objects pulling on other objects. The force of gravity between two objects depends on their mass and how close they are to each other. Most objects don't pull on each other enough to measure. But Earth is a massive object. The force between it and other objects is powerful. Gravity pulls so hard that it holds objects down on Earth's surface, even though Earth is spinning.

The force between you and Earth is holding you where you are. If you jump into the air, the force of gravity will pull you back down. Without Earth's gravity, everything would go flying off into space.

Astronauts floating in *Atlantis* space shuttle

How would this picture be different if the space shuttle were parked on Earth?

Did you know that the games you play depend on forces? How would your favorite game be different without gravity?

Weight

Gravity pulls you down all the time. When you step on a bathroom scale, the scale shows the strength of the pull. We call this pull your weight.

Weight is usually the same as the force of gravity on an object. When you stand still on a scale, the weight shown is the force of gravity that is pulling between you and Earth.

Your scale probably shows your weight in pounds. If the scale reads 55 pounds, the force of gravity pulling you down is 55 pounds. In the metric system, the unit that measures forces is the newton. A newton isn't as big as a pound, so you would weigh more in newtons than pounds. If you weighed 55 pounds, you'd weigh about 245 newtons.

TRY THIS

Activity!

Heavy Words

What You Need
string, book, spring scale, *Activity Log* page 12

How much does Earth pull on a book? Use string to hook a spring scale to a book. Hang the book over the floor. What does the spring scale read? Explain how this shows that Earth is pulling on the book.

Activity!

Packing Heavy Words

What is one way you feel pushes and pulls?

What You Need
backpack, books, piece of string, Activity Log page 13

Load the backpack with books. Carry it around the room once by its strap. Now, tie a piece of string to the backpack so you can pick it up. Carry the backpack around the room once using the string handle. Record how the two handles felt. How is the string different from the strap? Why was the string less comfortable?

Pressure

In the activity, the backpack weighed the same both times. It put the same force on your hand both times. The only difference was that one handle was wider. The strap spread the force over more of your hand.

What you felt was a difference in pressure (presh´ ər). **Pressure** measures the force pushing on an area. The string handle put all the weight of the backpack on a very small area. The strap spread the force over more of your hand. You didn't have as much force pressing down on just a small part of your hand.

 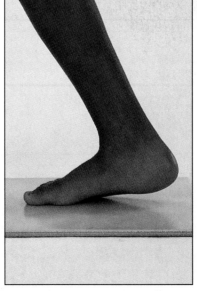

Pressure explains why it hurts to walk barefoot on small rocks. On a smooth surface, the force of your weight is spread out over the bottom of your feet. But when you step on small rocks, the force of your weight isn't spread out as much.

Printers used forces to print the book you are reading. How do you think they use pressure and pushes and pulls?

SCIENCE TECHNOLOGY AND Society

Focus on Technology

Start the Presses!

A press is a machine that prints books. It presses, or pushes down, on the paper. Before there were presses, people had to write every copy of a book by hand!

The oldest printed book in existence was printed in China.

The Chinese and Japanese people were the first to print books. They began thousands of years ago. Printers put ink on blocks with carved characters and pressed the blocks against paper. The blocks left ink on the paper in the shape of the characters.

People supplied the energy to run the first printing presses. Today, electricity supplies the energy to run huge printing presses that print up to 32 pages at once. Ink is pressed onto paper by large rollers.

Worth the Weight

Gravity is one of the most common pulls. Because gravity pulls almost exactly the same all around the world, many things are sold by weight. The more something weighs, the more you pay for it.

Minds On! At the grocery store, how many things are sold by weight? In your *Activity Log* on page 15, draw or make a list of things that you buy by weight. ●

Math **Link**

Weight in Gold

The saying "You're worth your weight in gold" comes from a book called *The Spy*, by James Fenimore Cooper. One of the characters said, "That animal is worth his weight in gold." What do you think the character was really saying about the animal? If someone gave you your weight in gold, how much money would that be? You can find the price of gold in the newspaper. Use your weight and the price to find how many dollars it would be.

Think about the kind of scales you have seen. Basket scales that weigh fruit at the grocery store work like the spring scale you've been using. They have a spring on the inside behind the big dial. An older kind of scale is the balance. It looks like the one on these pages. You know the weight of one thing. You put the weight of the thing you know on one side of the balance. Then you start to add weight to the other side. When the sides balance, you know the weight of both sides. They weigh the same.

Sum It Up

Forces are all around you. To do almost anything, you use forces to push or pull. Sometimes you use energy to create a force. You use another kind of force when you use a magnet or apply pressure. The force of gravity holds things down on Earth. Gravity is pulling on you and everything else on Earth all the time.

Critical Thinking

1. Gravity on Earth is six times stronger than gravity on the moon. How much would you weigh on the moon?
2. How can forces be working if things are not moving?
3. Is it easier to push a heavy object or to pull it? Why?

"Don't fight forces; use them."

— R. Buckminster Fuller

Buster Keaton in the 1927 film *The General*.

Is It Moving?

A train is a very large object. Making it move or stopping its movement takes a lot of force. You can't move a train. But when you move an object, you use the same forces it would take to move that train. You pull or you push. Sometimes this causes motion. Sometimes it does not. You could pull or push on a train that wasn't moving, but it still wouldn't move. Do you know why?

Minds On! Roll your pencil across your desk. Your push made it start rolling. What made it stop rolling? Write what you think in your *Activity Log* on page 16. ●

How can you slow down, speed up, or change the direction of motion? Think about this in the next Explore Activity when you work with forces to move a knot.

Activity!

Changing Motion

What do you have to do to change the movement of an object? In this activity, you will explore what is necessary to change motion.

What You Need

Activity Log pages 17-18

paper clips

string

masking tape

washers

scissors

What To Do

1 Cut four pieces of string that are as long as the width of your desk. Knot the ends of the four strings together so the strings make a big **X**. Tie a paper clip to the loose end of each string. Bend each paper clip to make a hook.

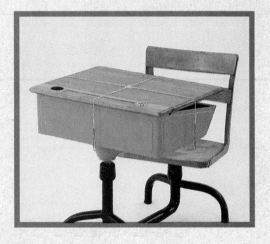

2 Mark the center of the desk with a small piece of masking tape. Place the big knot in the middle of the desk with one string hanging off each edge of the desk.

3 Have one person hold the center knot in place while another person hangs two washers on one paper clip hook. Predict what will happen if you let go of the center knot. Then test your prediction.

4 Take the two washers off. Make sure the knot is back in the center. Hold the knot in place. Add one washer to each of the four paper clip hooks.

5 Mark the starting position of the center knot on the diagram of your desk. Record how many washers are on each paper clip. Predict what to do to move the center knot near one corner of the desk.

6 Test your prediction. Hang one washer at a time on a paper clip. After you place each washer, mark the new position of the center knot with tape. Record the knot position and the number of washers on each paper clip on the diagram. Do this until you have moved the knot to one corner of the desk.

What Happened?

1. How did the position of the center knot compare to its position when there were two washers on each paper clip?

2. Why did the center knot move when you added the first washer? Why didn't the center knot move when you added a washer to each paper clip?

What Now?

1. How many washers were needed to move the center knot to a corner? Where were they placed? Compare results with another group. How were they alike? Different?

2. Why do you think the center knot moved to a corner?

3. How could you move the knot back to the middle?

EXPLORE

What Causes Motion?

In the Explore Activity, you observed that when something was not moving, you had to unbalance the forces holding it in place to make it move. When there was one washer on each string, the weight of each one was pulling equally on the center knot. Four forces were working on the knot at the same time. Because the forces were balanced, the knot didn't move.

Every time you pick something up, you're playing tug-of-war with the force of gravity.

When you put different amounts of weight on the strings, the forces didn't balance anymore. That's why the knot moved. The extra weight gave the knot a pull that was strong enough to unbalance the forces acting on it.

Every time you pick something up, you are unbalancing the forces on it. You are pulling up harder than gravity is pulling down. Pick up a ball from the floor, and you unbalance the forces on it. Hold the ball steady above the floor, and you balance the forces.

Minds On! Just like pulls, pushes can be balanced, too. Push both your hands together with the same force. Do your hands move? Now push one hand harder than the other. Your forces are now out of balance. What happens? ●

The forces on a moving object must be unbalanced to change its motion. It takes an added force to stop it, speed it up, or change its direction. Do the next Try This Activity to see how this works.

Activity!

Rolling Along

What You Need
table-tennis ball, *Activity Log* page 19

Using a force, you can change the direction of motion. Roll a table-tennis ball across your desk. While the ball is rolling, have another person blow on it from the side. Make a drawing of what happens. Now, roll the ball again and blow from the front and then the back. What happens? Record your observations.

Follow the path of the ball on this pinball machine. What changes to start the ball moving? What stops it? What changes its direction? Are the forces on the ball pushes or pulls?

Friction

You know that rolling balls always come to a stop. Even after rolling down a long hill, they slow down and stop. It takes force to make things slow down and stop. In the Try This Activity, you'll see an example of one common force that does this.

Workers building a roof.

Activity!

Rough or Smooth?

What You Need
smooth board, 3 wooden blocks, 4 thumbtacks, sandpaper, masking tape, *Activity Log* page 20

Cover the side of one block with sandpaper. Push the tacks into the four corners on one side of another block. **Safety Tip:** Use tacks carefully.

Line up all three blocks on one end of the board. The blocks with sandpaper or tacks should have that side down. Raise the end of the wood to make a ramp. Which block moves first? Which one moves last? Why didn't all the blocks move as soon as you started to raise the board?

In the Try This Activity, gravity started pulling the blocks down the board as soon as you started to lift it. They didn't begin to move right away because of friction (frik´ shən). **Friction** is the force that acts against motion when two surfaces are touching. Friction held the objects in place at first.

As the ramp became steeper, the force of gravity down the ramp became stronger. The force of gravity finally was stronger than the force of the friction. One block moved before the others because rough surfaces cause more friction than smooth ones do.

Friction is something you use every day. Without friction, you couldn't walk. Your feet couldn't push against the ground. You couldn't even turn the knob on a door to open it.

What would happen in each picture if there were no friction?

Rock climbers in Eldorado Canyon, Colorado

Inertia

There is something that resists, or works against, any change in motion, even if the objects are not touching. **Inertia** (in ûr´ shə) is what makes objects resist changes in motion. Objects that are not moving remain still unless an unbalanced force acts on them. When an object is not moving, you need to pull it or push it to make it move.

Inertia is also what keeps objects moving. Until an unbalanced force like friction acts on it, a moving object will not stop.

Pretend you're in space, with no planets near you. If you leap forward, you will keep going forever in the same direction because of inertia, unless another force acts on you. On Earth, gravity and friction usually combine to stop moving objects, like this skate.

TRY THIS

Activity!

Buckle Up!

What You Need
toy truck, wooden block, 3-m string, *Activity Log* page 21

Put the block in the bed of the truck. Tie the string to the truck. Predict what will happen to the block if your partner rolls the truck at high speed while you hold the string. Do the experiment and record your observations.

In the Try This Activity, inertia kept the truck moving after it was pushed. Inertia also kept the block moving after the string stopped the truck. You've probably felt the effects of inertia yourself. When a car starts, you feel pushed back into the seat because the effect of inertia makes you stay still. When a car stops, you feel pulled forward because the effect of inertia makes you keep moving.

Staying Safe

You can be badly hurt if you are riding in a car that stops suddenly. Inertia keeps your body going until something stops it. If an air bag or seat belt stops your body, you will be hurt less than if the windshield stops you. Most states now have laws about wearing seat belts. But some people still don't wear them.

Many people are trying to make sure air bags are in every car. Air bags work automatically. But they don't take the place of a seat belt. Air bags save lives, but they are expensive.

Do you wear a seat belt every time you ride in a car? Do you think air bags are a good idea? Are they worth the money?

Controlling Friction

If something is wet, it can be more slippery. You know that some shoes can make you slip on a waxed floor. What would happen if your feet flew out from under you whenever you tried to walk? Not having enough friction can be a real problem.

There are many ways to increase friction. Roads should have rough surfaces to help keep tires from slipping when it rains. What other ways do we increase friction to keep people safe?

Wet roads can be dangerous.

Too much friction can be a problem, too. Rub your hands together. With a little motion and friction, you made heat. When there is too much friction in machines, moving parts can get very hot. This can damage the machines. Slippery oil reduces friction between moving parts.

Big machines, such as cars, have pipes and tubes to get oil where it's needed. Have you seen someone add oil to a car?

Safety Check

Do a safety check of your school. Observe ways that controlling friction makes it a safer, more comfortable place to be. With a small group, record on page 22 in your *Activity Log* the examples that you observed. Invite your custodian to class to tell you about additional things that are done to control friction at school.

Sum It Up

Even if nothing is moving, forces are acting on you and the objects around you. When you unbalance these forces, you make things move. You have to overcome other forces like friction to start and keep things moving. Without friction, it would be harder to stop things. Because of inertia, things tend to stay the way they are until some force acts on them.

Critical Thinking

1. Which is stronger—gravity's pull or the pull you use to lift a book? How do you know?
2. How could you make a toy race car go faster? How can you make it go further?
3. Why don't you ice skate on concrete? Why don't you roller skate on ice?

Here are some riddles. When can you pull or push down to lift something up? When can you turn something to lift something? When do you push in to push out? By the end of this lesson, you'll know the answers.

Stan Laurel and Oliver Hardy in the 1938 film *Swiss Miss.*

Machines and Work

What machines have you used today? Probably many, many more than you think. Every day you use machines as you play and work. They can help you make forces more useful by changing pushes to pulls. Machines make our lives easier. They help us do things we can't do on our own.

Minds On! Suppose you wanted to move a piano into a truck. No matter how hard you push or pull, you can't lift it. On page 23 in your **Activity Log,** write a plan to solve the problem. ●

Some machines are big, loud, and expensive. Others are very simple. And believe it or not, it's the simple ones we use the most. In the next Explore Activity, you'll make one of these simple machines to solve a problem.

Activity!

Need a Lift?

You know that forces can be used to move objects. Sometimes we want to move an object that takes a lot of force to move. How can we do it? In this activity, you will make a machine that will move an object.

What You Need

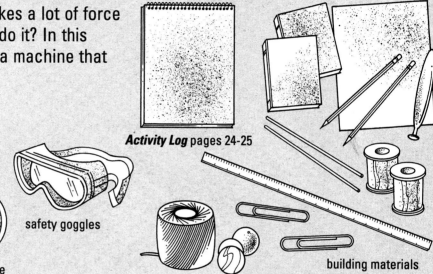

Activity Log pages 24-25

scissors

masking tape

safety goggles

building materials

What To Do

1 Invent a way to get the roll of tape from the floor to your desk top. You can use your hands to provide the lift. But you can't just pick up the tape and put it on the desk.

2 With your group, think of as many different ways as you can to lift the tape. Then, plan two different ways to get the tape to the top of the desk. Write or draw your ideas in your *Activity Log*.

Safety!

See the *Safety Tip* in step 3.

3 Show your plans to your teacher. After your teacher has approved your plans, try one of them. *Safety Tip:* Wear safety goggles if you are using rubber bands. Write what happens in your **Activity Log**. If it didn't work well, what went wrong? What could you do to fix it?

4 Try your other plan for lifting the tape. Write what happens this time.

5 Discuss your other ideas with your teacher. Then try each of them. Write down the result each time.

What Happened?

1. How many ways did you come up with to raise the tape to the top of your desk? Which one worked the best?

2. What materials did you use?

3. What forces did you use?

What Now?

1. Why didn't some of your ideas work as well as others?

2. Which idea required the least amount of effort to do?

EXPLORE

Using Machines

You probably invented many different ways of getting the tape to your desk top. Maybe you tried several ways before you found one that worked. That's what inventors, scientists, and engineers do. To solve a problem, they keep trying. And they learn as much from what doesn't work as they do from what does work.

When you moved the tape to the desk top, you had to use a tool or an object to help you. You probably invented a machine. A **machine** is a tool used to change a force.

Machines make work seem easier. Who do you think is doing work in this picture?

Work has a special meaning in science. **Work** is done when a force acts on an object and moves it over a distance. Now, look at this picture as a scientist. Who is doing work? Who isn't doing work?

Minds On! Pick up your pencil. Put it down. Did you do some work? Why? Now, push down hard on your desk. Did your hand or the desk move? Did you do some work? Why? ●

You used force to move your pencil over a distance. That's why you did work on the pencil. When you pushed down on your desk, you did no work. If an object doesn't move, no work is done. It doesn't matter how hard you push or pull it.

With machines we can do many things we couldn't do with just our own muscles. A **simple machine** is a machine that has few moving parts. Some have no moving parts.

Machines don't put out more work than we put into them. But they do change the amount of force, its direction, and the distance over which it acts.

On the next pages, you'll find out about some simple machines. And you'll see how a family uses them to build a tree house.

Simple Machines

There are three simple machines that are based on an inclined plane (in klīnd´ plān). *Inclined* means "at a slant" and *plane* means "flat surface." An **inclined plane** is a flat surface that is higher at one end.

A ramp is a kind of inclined plane. Every time you use a ramp, you are using an inclined plane. Where is the inclined plane in the picture?

Focus on Technology

Going Up?

Have you seen long, slanted walkways going up beside the stairs in some buildings? People using wheelchairs or baby strollers use these inclined planes to climb to the door. On a ramp, it doesn't take as strong a force to move a few inches as it does to go up a step. Laws now require public buildings to provide ramps. Do you think this is a good idea? Why or why not?

TRY THIS Activity!

Splitting Up

What else can an inclined plane do?

What You Need

wooden door stop, stack of books, *Activity Log* page 26

Use your hands like bookends, and hold the books up on your desk. Have another person put the narrow end of the doorstop between two books, and push gently. Describe in your ***Activity Log*** what you see and feel as the other person pushes.

An inclined plane used to push things apart is called a **wedge** (wej). A doorstop works as a wedge. When someone peels potatoes, the knife is a wedge. It pushes the skin apart from the rest of the potato. Where is the wedge in this picture?

Another simple machine is a screw (skrü). A **screw** is an inclined plane that winds around into a spiral. Screws are usually used to hold things together. When you tighten the lid on a jar, you are using a screw. What's another example you see in this picture?

More Simple Machines

Activity!

One-finger Lift

How do you lift something that's heavy?

What You Need

wooden ruler, pencil, heavy book, *Activity Log* page 27

Place the book on the end of the ruler. Lift the ruler and put the pencil under the middle. Press down to lift the book. Now, try the same thing with the pencil closer and farther from the book. Draw the way that seemed easiest and the way that seemed hardest.

In the activity, you used a ruler and a pencil as a lever (lev´ ər). A **lever** is an arm that turns around a point. The lever arm was your ruler. The point the lever turns on is called the **fulcrum** (fül´ krəm). Your pencil was the fulcrum. There are two other simple machines that are kinds of levers.

It's easier to lift a very heavy object or pry something up with a lever than it is without one. Tools that can pry or pull things up are levers. Where is the lever that is prying something up in this picture?

Another kind of lever is a wheel and axle (ak´ səl). A **wheel and axle** is a simple machine with a wheel that turns a post. The post is called an axle. Many common objects use a wheel and axle. A doorknob pulls the latch with a wheel and axle. How many wheels do you see in this picture? Which ones are part of a wheel and axle?

A third kind of lever is a pulley (pŭl´ ē). A **pulley** is a simple machine in which a rope fits around a wheel. A pulley is often used to lift things. It lets you stand on the ground and pull a rope down to lift something up. Where is the pulley in this picture?

A **compound machine** is made up of two or more simple machines that are connected. Two of the simple machines in this picture are working together as a compound machine. Can you find it?

Energy and Machines

Machines can't do work by themselves. However, by doing work, they transfer energy from one thing or system to another. Energy is the ability to do work. A machine can't transfer any more energy than you put into it. When you use a simple machine, it is probably getting its energy from you. You get energy from food.

For a long time, people used only simple machines to help them. People provided the energy that was needed.

Building in ancient Egypt

Silver and goldsmithing equipment

▲About 200 years ago, many machines were invented for making lots of different things. The machines used energy from burning coal or wood to do work.

▼Today many machines use electricity to work. Electricity comes into homes and other buildings from big power plants. At some power plants, energy from burning coal or oil is used to make electricity.

Coal-fired power plant

▲You use machines every day of your life. What one is being used in this picture?

Literature 🔗 Link

The Berenstain Bears' Science Fair
by Stan and Jan Berenstain

In your *Activity Log* on page 28, make a list or draw pictures of ten machines you find in the pictures in this book. Compare lists with your classmates. What forces make the machines work? From where do they get energy?

Sum It Up

Look back to the beginning of this lesson. To lift a piano, you could use simple machines to change forces. You could push down on a lever to lift it up. You could try to push it up an inclined plane. You could even build a wheel and axle machine to pull it up. The way machines work lets us do more things more easily.

Critical Thinking

1. Suppose you pick up a piece of paper and your friend tries to lift a car, but can't. Who is doing more work? Why?

2. Using what you have learned, how would you answer the riddles on page 48?

3. How can you make a pencil act as a wedge? As a lever? As an inclined plane?

Bumper cars, Riyadh Amusement Park,
Saudi Arabia

Fun With Forces and Machines

In all the excitement at an amusement
park, you may not ever notice the forces
and machines that are there. Look
carefully at the pictures. Everything is
frozen in position. Find three things that
change position in the next minute. From
where do you think these machines are
getting energy?

Mount Tom Summerslide, Holyoke, MA

Minds On! In your
Activity Log
on page 29, draw a ride
you like or one from your
imagination that shows
each of the characteristics
below.

- machine that has
  overcome the force of
  friction to move fast
- machine that uses
  friction to slow down ●

Ferris wheel,
Coney Island,
NY ▶

Super swings, Pützchens Markt, Germany

Flying cars,
Barcelona,
Spain ▶

Skyjump,
Knott's Berry
Farm, Buena
Vista, CA

Looking Inside: Machines and Constructions

by Paul Fleisher and Patricia A. Keeler.

On page 30 in your *Activity Log,* make a list of simple machines that are part of the larger machines you see in this book. Put a check mark next to the ones that you have used. Do you push, pull, or turn something to use each one?

TRY THIS Activity!

Your Own Amusement Park

With a small group of classmates, design your own amusement park. Use what you've learned about forces and machines in this unit to build models of rides and other amusements for your park. Below are some materials you might like to use. You may think of others.

Suggested Materials
balls of different sizes, straws, short boards, small spools, paper plates, the bottoms from small milk cartons, pencils, craft sticks, glue, tape, paper fasteners, crayons, cardboard, scissors, butcher paper, safety goggles, *Activity Log* page 31

1. Begin by planning your amusement park with your group. Use your *Activity Log* to write down ideas.

2. Decide on a game or a ride you would like to make for your miniature amusement park. Decide what kind of machines you will use. Make a drawing or plan in your *Activity Log*.

3. Make a list of all the materials you will need to make your ride or game. Then, find the materials and make it. *Safety Tip:* Wear safety goggles if you use rubber bands.

4. What type of machine did you use in your ride or game? What type of force has to be unbalanced to make it move? Compare your ride or game with those of your classmates. Which one moves the fastest? Why?

5. Put your amusement park together on a big piece of butcher paper. Draw in some roads, grass, and trees for your park. Share your amusement park with a group of younger students.

In a way, the world is like a big amusement park. There are forces and machines everywhere. Energy and forces together make things move. Long ago, people had just a few simple machines to help them. Today, there are very complicated ones. Maybe you will invent a machine that will make life on Earth even easier.

GLOSSARY

Use the pronunciation key below to help you decode, or read, the pronunciations.

Pronunciation Key

a	at, bad	d	dear, soda, bad
ā	ape, pain, day, break	f	five, defend, leaf, off, cough, elephant
ä	father, car, heart	g	game, ago, fog, egg
âr	care, pair, bear, their, where	h	hat, ahead
e	end, pet, said, heaven, friend	hw	white, whether, which
ē	equal, me, feet, team, piece, key	j	joke, enjoy, gem, page, edge
i	it, big, English, hymn	k	kite, bakery, seek, tack, cat
ī	ice, fine, lie, my	l	lid, sailor, feel, ball, allow
îr	ear, deer, here, pierce	m	man, family, dream
o	odd, hot, watch	n	not, final, pan, knife
ō	old, oat, toe, low	ng	long, singer, pink
ô	coffee, all, taught, law, fought	p	pail, repair, soap, happy
ôr	order, fork, horse, story, pour	r	ride, parent, wear, more, marry
oi	oil, toy	s	sit, aside, pets, cent, pass
ou	out, now	sh	shoe, washer, fish mission, nation
u	up, mud, love, double	t	tag, pretend, fat, button, dressed
ū	use, mule, cue, feud, few	th	thin, panther, both
ü	rule, true, food	th	this, mother, smooth
ù	put, wood, should	v	very, favor, wave
ûr	burn, hurry, term, bird, word, courage	w	wet, weather, reward
ə	about, taken, pencil, lemon, circus	y	yes, onion
b	bat, above, job	z	zoo, lazy, jazz, rose, dogs, houses
ch	chin, such, match	zh	vision, treasure, seizure

compound machine (kom´pound mə shēn´) a machine made up of two or more simple machines

energy (en´ər jē) the ability to exert a force and make something move. Energy is the ability to do work.

force (fôrs) something that causes an object to move, or to change or stop its motion. A force is a push or pull.

friction (frik´shən) the force that acts against motion when two surfaces are touching. Friction slows down or stops objects in motion.

fulcrum (fùl´krəm) the point where a lever rocks back and forth

gravity (grav´i tē) the pulling force between two objects. The force of gravity between two objects depends on their mass and how close they are to each other.

inclined plane (in klīnd´ plān) a simple machine used to move objects to a higher or lower place. A ramp is an example of an inclined plane.

inertia (in ûr´shə) the property of objects that resists change in motion. Objects that are not moving remain still unless an unbalanced force acts on them. Objects keep moving in straight lines unless a force acts on them.

lever (lev´ər) a simple machine that can be used to raise or lower an object

machine (mə shēn´) a tool used to change a force

mass (mas) the amount of matter in an object

motion (mō´shən) the process of changing position or place

newton (nü´tən) the metric unit that measures forces. A newton isn't as big as a pound, so you would weigh more in newtons than pounds.

position (pə zish´ən) the place where a person or thing is

pressure (presh´ər) the measure of a force pushing on an area

pulley (pŭl´ē) a simple machine consisting of a wheel and a rope or cable. A pulley changes the direction or amount of a force.

screw (skrü) a simple machine that is an inclined plane wrapped around a post

simple machine (sim´ pəl mə shēn´) a machine that has few or no moving parts

speed (spēd) how fast an object moves

wedge (wej) a solid triangular or tapered piece of wood or metal that can be used to separate, split, or lift objects

weight (wāt) the measure of the force of gravity on an object that is not moving

wheel and axle (whēl and ak´ səl) a simple machine with a wheel attached to a position bar called an axle. Turning the wheel turns the axle.

work (wûrk) what is done when a force moves an object

INDEX

CREDITS

Photo Credits:

Cover, The Image Bank/Geoffrey Gove; **1,** ©KS Studios; **2,3,** (m) ©Stuart Cohen/Comstock, Inc.; **3,** ©KS Studios; **4,** ©Studiohio; **8,** (t) Gerald L. French/FPG International, (m) Lee Balterman/FPG International, (b) The Image Bank/Alan Becker; **9,** (t) Duomo/Win McName, (m), (bl), (br) ©KS Studios/1991; **10,** ©Studiohio; **11,** ©Studiohio; **12,** Mike Powell/Allsport; **14,** ©KS Studios/1991; **15,** ©KS Studios/1991; **16,** Duomo/David Madison; **18,** (l) Bruce Coleman Inc./Bob & Clara Calhoun; (b) David Young-Wolff/PhotoEdit; **18,19,** Zephyr Pictures/Reed Koestner; **20,** ©Tim Courlas; **20, 21,** UNIPHOTO; **24, 25,** ©KS Studios/1991; **26,** ©KS Studios/1991; **27,** ©KS Studios/1991; **30,** NASA; **31,** ©KS Studios/1991; **32,** (l) © KS Studios/1991; (r) ©KS Studios/1991; **33,** British Library; **34, 35,** ©Studiohio; **36,37,** The Kobal Collection/Superstock; **38,** ©KS Studios/1991; **39,** ©KS Studios/1991; **40,** ©Studiohio; **43,** (t) David Lissy/West Stock, (b) Susan Van Etten/PhotoEdit; **44,45,** Duomo; **45,** (b) National Highway Safety Administration; **46,** (t) UNIPHOTO, (b) Richard Haynes/RM International Photography; **48, 49,** Nawrocki Stock Photo, Inc.; **58,** (t) Historical Pictures Service, (m) Jeri Gleiter/FPG International, (b) ©Brent Turner/BLT Productions/1991; **60,** (t) Jane Lewis/Tony Stone Worldwide/Chicago Ltd., (b) ©Comstock, Inc.; **61,** (t) Randy Duchaine/The Stock Market **60, 61,** Tony Stone Worldwide/Chicago Ltd. (br) ©Stuart Cohen/Comstock, Inc., (bl) Michelle Burgess/The Stock Market

Illustration Credits:

6, 7, Ron Himler; **14, 26, 38, 50,** Bob Giuliani; **16, 17,** James Shough; **17(t),** Thomas Kennedy; **20, 41, 46,** Ian Greathead; **22, 23,** Susan Moore; **28, 29, 52-57,** Eldon Doty, **58,** Alan Eitzen